SWAMP

WALKING THE WETLANDS OF THE SWAN COASTAL PLAIN

Nandi Chinna was born in Adelaide in 1964. She spent seven years living in yoga ashrams in NSW and Victoria before moving to Perth in 1990. She has worked as a gardener, organic farmer, school teacher, disability support worker, journalist, actor and teacher of creative writing. Her poetry has been widely published in national and international journals and anthologies and has been broadcast on RTRFM and 6PR local radio in Perth, and on ABC Radio National's *Poetica*. Her first collection of poetry *Our Only Guide is Our Homesickness* was published in the Five Islands Press New Poets publishing program in 2007. Her chap book *How to Measure Land* won the Byron Bay Writers Festival Picaro Poetry prize in 2010. Nandi's passions and interests include walking wild, encounters with non-human species, swamps, spaces of dereliction and beauty, and seeking way better ways to live in mutuality with our Earth home.

Visit Nandi at **swampwalking.com.au**.

Aboriginal and Torres Strait Islander people are respectfully advised that deceased people are referenced in this publication.

SWAMP

WALKING THE WETLANDS OF
THE SWAN COASTAL PLAIN

NANDI CHINNA

FREMANTLE PRESS

It is through the lake system. There is a water serpent down there below which is extremely important and the water on the surface is really the marks where the waugle wither wound his way through and came up after making the streams and the waterways. It's all part of the ecological system to purify the land and the family. Once it was surrounded by waterways and if they fill them up with rubbish then the land begins to die.

Cedric Jacobs

A lake is the landscape's most beautiful and expressive feature. It is earth's eye; looking into which the beholder measures the depth of his own nature.

Henry David Thoreau

CONTENTS

Introduction – Swamp Walking

I shall never understand, how it can be called a pleasure to hurtle past all the images and objects which our beautiful earth displays, as if one had gone mad and had to accelerate for fear of despair.

Robert Walser

Walking; putting one foot in front of the other, poising the weight on one foot and then tilting the body forward with the other foot, swinging this foot in front of the body and placing it on the ground in front of you to prevent falling. Walking reconstructs Galileo's pendulum, the legs move through time and space, marking the movement over grass, stones, hills, and through wind which is air moving through space. I walk slowly and time dissipates to the stillness of my breath wrapping around me in tight coils. As I pick up speed, time gathers to meet me, rushing around the curvature of the Earth.

For the creative practitioner, walking reintroduces the body as a fundamental definer of experience. The walker uses the body as a 'divining rod', pacing through time and the city, noticing what demands to be noticed, and stitching together maps which link sense perceptions with histories in order to build a greater dimension into the narrative that defines place. As Rebecca Solnit observes in her history of walking, 'exploring the world is one of the best ways of exploring the mind, and walking travels both terrains' [1].

From March 2009 until March 2012 I undertook a series of walks in and around Perth's drained and buried wetlands as well as those remnant wetlands which still exist and which offer a reference point to the swampy history of the Swan Coastal Plain. I walked twice, often three times per week in the first eighteen months, which reduced to two walks per week in the latter half of the project. I wore out two pairs of walking shoes and made a significant impact upon a third pair.

Walking the shores of Perth's lakes becomes a radical activity when we consider that most of these wetland lakes are now buried beneath the roads and buildings of the metropolitan area. In these times of water restrictions and desalination plants it may surprise many present day residents of Perth to discover that the Swan Coastal Plain, where Perth city is located, was once characterised by complex chains and suites of wetlands, fed by fresh springs and underwater aquifers. Perth was once a seasonally wet place with an abundance of fresh water.

In order to find the lost wetland lakes, I placed new maps of Perth over old maps, maps which are sometimes just plans of the city-to-be. Here the soft blurred shapes of lakes, the traced outline of phantom water bodies, are just visible beneath the surveyor's straight lines and grids.

In the spirit of the psychogeographers, my walks were planned in as much as the starting points were defined but I also maintained an openness which allowed me to stumble across the unexpected – Walter's Brook flowing beneath back lanes, its sound and smell emanating from an open drain vent – and to change direction if the terrain dictated it, to follow birds, and paths made by walking, to have encounters with people and wildlife, and sometimes to wander too far and too long resulting in sore feet and weary countenance. My walks were most often conducted at a slow pace, and could more be described as a ramble, amble or as it is beautifully expressed in Noongar language, a '*yannow*; to saunter; to walk; to move slowly along' [2]. This kind of walking is also closely aligned with the idea of the psychogeographical *dérive* translated literally as 'drift', or what Alistair Bonnett calls 'politically purposeful drifting' [3]. Where possible I used my bicycle and/or public transport to reach the beginning of my walks, and this too became part of the journey, across the country of my enquiry, to the historical country beneath.

In my walking practice my research tools are my body and my imagination. I try as much as possible to use all my senses in my enquiry. Walking also involves sitting in places and engaging in deep listening, exploring the layers of sound from the loudest to the barely perceptible. It involves tasting plants, water and air, touching these same; noticing wind currents, movements of birds and people, and all the colliding and conflicting sensations that the body experiences in an environment. I record my observations in a series of notebooks, and use these notes to later inform the poems I write.

Poetry contains both rational and irrational elements. For Edward Hirsch, poetry shoulders 'the burden of the mystery' [4] and can be at once illuminating yet casting its own shadows. Poetry perhaps offers another, deeper perspective upon sets of events which situate us in time and space and help us to understand where we are. Matthew Cooperman reflects that 'in leading us ever on and in, a poem clears a space for contemplation and action; it gathers utility as a vehicle of imminent clearing' [5]. To define my walking/writing practice I constructed the neologism *poepatetics* or the poetry of walking: *poe* from poesis or making; *patetics* from peripatetics or walking, travelling; a person who walks and travels about [6]. More simply put, poepatetics is 'making from walking'. Poepatetics is a combination of three disciplines: the observed phenomena, the subjective bodily experience, and transcription of both the tangible and enigmatic into text.

Poepatetics has a long history reflected in the poetry of Mastuo Basho in the seventeenth century through to Wordsworth, Dickens, Whitman, Thoreau, Wallace Stevens, Robert Walser, and more recently W. G. Sebald, Rebecca Solnit, Mary Oliver and Gary Snyder, all of whom are walker-writers whose work reflects the drive of homesickness for the wild, and for beings other than human.

The production of the poems in this work is closely related to the walking practice; it is the physical experience of the places in which I walk that really provides the basis for most of the pieces. Even the historical poems are informed by my walking knowledge of the terrain and my intimacy with wetlands that exist today.

These walks in wetlands provide me with a way of imagining how things were for the newcomers who came to encounter, misunderstand and ultimately destroy most of the swamps on the Swan Coastal Plain

When I examine my own motivations for writing about the lost lakes of Perth, I come to see that my forays in the city and the resulting poems are motivated by a sense of grief over the loss of local and global ecosystems and the escalating rate of species extinctions. The black birds that fly overhead as I walk — the Carnaby's cockatoo and the forest red-tailed cockatoo — are two such species that, due to land clearing and climate change, are predicted to become extinct within the next fifty years [7]. The wetlands that remain as remnants on the Swan Coastal Plain are disappearing as my pen scrawls across the page, due to continuing urban development, altered hydrology and climate change [8]. The walking project is an attempt to find a horizon within this dialogue of loss, and within the altered geography of local and global environments.

In *Openings: A Meditation of History, Method, and Sumas Lake*, Anne Cameron suggests that whilst many people are aware that global environments are facing unprecedented degradation, a deeper, more important issue is the 'real human capacity to forget a disappeared environment' [9]. When a landscape such as the Swan Coastal Plain has been so thoroughly altered and re-engineered, the flora, fauna, lakes and rivers that connect people to the history and stories of a place are easily forgotten. Cameron argues that 'perhaps one purpose of history is to make people miss what they haven't experienced and to help them understand where they are'. It is in this spirit that I have utilised the methodologies of the Situationists who developed psychogeography, harnessing in particular what Bonnett describes as an 'uprooted nostalgia: a free-floating sense of loss that presents permanent marginality' [10], and what Albrecht calls 'solastalgia,' the homesickness induced by radical change in a home place [11]. I do so in order to address the loss of the wetlands of the Swan Coastal Plain as a metaphor for wider global losses of environments and the non-human life that has disappeared with them.

As poepatetics practitioner Robert Walser explains in his short story 'The Walk':

> Walk ... I definitely must, to invigorate myself and to maintain contact with the living world, without perceiving which I could not write the half of one more single word, or produce the tiniest poem in verse or prose. Without walking, I would be dead, and my profession, which I love passionately, would be destroyed. [12]

For me the walk is essential to the creative process, both as a lyrical meter, a bodily metronome, and as a way of perceiving the writer's connection and relation to the world in which they live. As I step out of my house on the west coast of Australia, near Fremantle, the south-westerly wind is sweeping across the park, depositing a fine taste of salt on my skin and tongue. My body shifts inside my clothes, stiff and slow to get moving. My feet, encased in light shoes, roll along the contours of rough ground. A bank of cloud hovers above the ridge to the west, where a flock of black Carnaby's cockatoos is reeling and wee-looing. I gain momentum, striding across the ragged grass that sews a fine covering across the history of this ground. My elderly neighbour remembers this ground as a swamp where Noongar people camped. She recalls walking along the edge of the swamp, past their camp on her way to the bus stop on Rockingham Road. My friend Tim remembers playing here in the 1960s, launching a homemade corrugated iron canoe between reeds into black water. I am walking through space that is also time and history. The stories enter my stride as I walk and are recorded on the map that is being walked into my body.

Boojoormelup – Lake Henderson, 1864 *[1]*

Writing on Water

First you must wade through the minutiae
copepods, water boatman, and backswimmers.
You may be bitten by fleas
reborn after aestivating for two hundred years.
Remember frogs cannot swallow
with their eyes open so they may not see you coming.
Sift out the sediment. (This can be achieved by taking off
your shirt and straining the water through the cloth.)
There is a lot to know before you can start:
water can kill as easily as quench,
water can be very old;
water makes ink run,
will dissolve paper.
One letter too many or too few
can change the whole meaning.
Until it dries out you may not be able to understand
what water has to say.

A Line Made by Walking

after Richard Long

How many footsteps will it take
to walk a place into the body?

From back door to garden, around each raised bed,
pressing a pad through harvest and fallow.

Beyond the front gate, countless ambulations
scorn footpaths, traverse weedy verges,
pace a cartography of desire
into the neighbourhood.

How many footsteps will it take
to trample grass stems, crush flowers
make a line by walking?

Boardwalk

Walking on water;
under canopies of paperbark and flower,
reed beds lean with the prevailing wind,
seeds drift west like a plague of insects.
The sound of footsteps on pine boards,
whirr of a camera deconstructing and re-authoring,
the lens seeks movement and finds subterfuge:
rustling and clicking, reed stems seem to turn their backs,
a tree branch quivers, the pond surface breaks all exits.

Mud Pie

Water was the first being;
then alluvium came without trace or mark,
before Kronos when the world
was still a cold mud pie,
any event pressed into it
later reads as history.

Cut yourself a piece and bite;
it'll taste like salt, like bodily fluids,
sparks will turn in an upward drift
forming wings, legs, whole arks
full of species illuminating the night.

Dead for years,
their lights still flicker
through the cycle of turning;
and trick us into believing that we know where we are,
that all we see passing will return again.

The City

A great abundance of fresh water of the best quality.

Charles Fraser, 1827 [1]

A scratch in the sand reveals fresh inundations,
mosquitoes are most peculiarly intimate,
swans can be plucked like black lilies
blooming in shallow reed beds.

Here is the place;
to stretch linen and rope across
the littoral where mudflats prevent the ocean
from swallowing the river.

This could be the future in two dimensions,
Between here and Mt Eliza tendrils of smoke
smudge the view, springs bleed south
beneath ink line drawings
of the imminent, the unborn city.

*I have just returned from (Perth) ... Not a blade of grass to be seen —
nothing but sand, scrub, shrubs and stunted trees from the verge of the
river to the tops of the hills ... The soil is such, on which no human being
can possibly exist.*

Samuel Taylor, 1830 [2]

Mounts Bay Road, Perth, c. 1870 *[2]*

*We had an excursion to Perth ... such a comfortless hole. The miserable
huts are built of wood on a soil of dark-coloured sand swarming with fleas
and mosquitoes. A more perfect purgatory could not be devised.*

Sydney Gazette, January 1830

Shoes

George Fletcher Moore's Found Poem [3]

No object to steer by
except your own shadow
moving as you move,
perplexing motion.

Boot leather enacts
the principles of increase and decay:
cracks open at the toe line,
with each step the parched sole
wounds back into porous skin.

Every two or three weeks
lace and tongue return to soil;
there is a great shortage of shoes
in the whole colony.

Sinking a Well, 1832

A scrape in the ground 2 feet deep
is level with the summer sunk swamp.
Beneath the ground's skein
the country tells its story in layers:
vegetable mould, blue and black clay,
white or dun clay, buff loamy clay,
yellow sandy loam, dun loamy sand.

Water at 12 feet,
brackish but suitable for washing.
Potable at 16 feet, cool and sapid:
place your lips to the tea-stained hole
and suck.

Boundaries

Eucalyptus rudis, flooded gum

*When the last two trees were struck with an axe, for the purpose of
making a boundary mark — a jet d'eau issued from out of a blue gum tree,
and continued running without intermission during the time of our stay —
a quarter of an hour. This water had a strong chalybeate taste.*

George Fletcher Moore [3]

A fountain of subterranean creek water
sieved through stones and gravel,
pumped through sun-punched leaves
turned sideways to shade their faces

Below the surface old rain
edges towards air, revolves
on this endless circuit;
seeps through canvas bags,
rusts the cloth of shirts.

In a land with no corners
the fence posts are alive;
their bark peels like skin, their sap
soaks mouths, bites tongues.

Swan River Fish, 14th September 1832

Fish numerous in the river about and below Perth. I mentioned our having taken 10 000 at one draught of the seine.

George Fletcher Moore [3]

We dip our oars in the wake of morning
stroking rings in an auric surface,
beneath our longing mullet ride,
grazing weed in the turn of tide.

Salt diffuses into sweetness,
flutes the river up to Guildford,
a gallimaufry of fish leaping,
surges into calloused weaving.

From the tangle of the river's body
every fish is a mouthful breaching,
hauled across the transom's line,
shattered scale and opaque eye;

a silver pile heaped on the bank:
kingy, snapper, mullet, perch,
cobbler's blade and darkening twist,
the jagged spines of Swan River fish.

The sunlight's cast upon the river
seals the furrows of our keel;
we count and stitch our catch in threes,
fish-shaped lanterns hang from trees.

Kingsford's Mill in Perth

Mr Kingsford proposes to cut a deep trench and lay a pipe from some
lagoons behind Perth, into the town to afford him a good supply of water.
George Fletcher Moore [3]

February spikes the afternoon into evening;
frogs entomb themselves
in the peat of the swamp
like an emperor's clay army.

Wedged between god and mortal,
lungs barely whisper,
for months or years in deep meditation
suspending all thought of
caddis fly, mosquito, and spawn.

A percussion of boot steps
wakes the sleeping amphibians;
shovel blades and crowbars
void them through the flume,
churning mill wheels
into their next incarnation.

1862

The sky is breaking, draining clouds,
pinging against unfamiliar rooftops,
insisting its way to the lowest point
and then raising its skirts higher.
The river spills from karstic furrows,
opens the ground in a wide brown gash.
Fish eggs hatch from muddy nests,
glaucomic tadpoles make their way across town,
their frogselves singing from newly formed ponds.
Rows of cabbages and potatoes
drift from their moorings,
a flock of great cormorants perched on the fence line,
sing transformation — farmland to lake.

The Ghost Road

Njookenbooroo – Herdsman Lake

The cartographer is not a boatman,
dipping his paddle amongst spinning ducks,
while companionable swans gaggle
in the centre of his calculations.

Beyond his sight a swamp harrier quarters the fringes,
scoping the undulations of sedge and reeds.
Coots dive and emerge again
at the opposite end of measure.

A line drawn on water cannot be transcribed
into chains, perches, miles;
its equations are dismantled
by the punting scull of webbed feet.

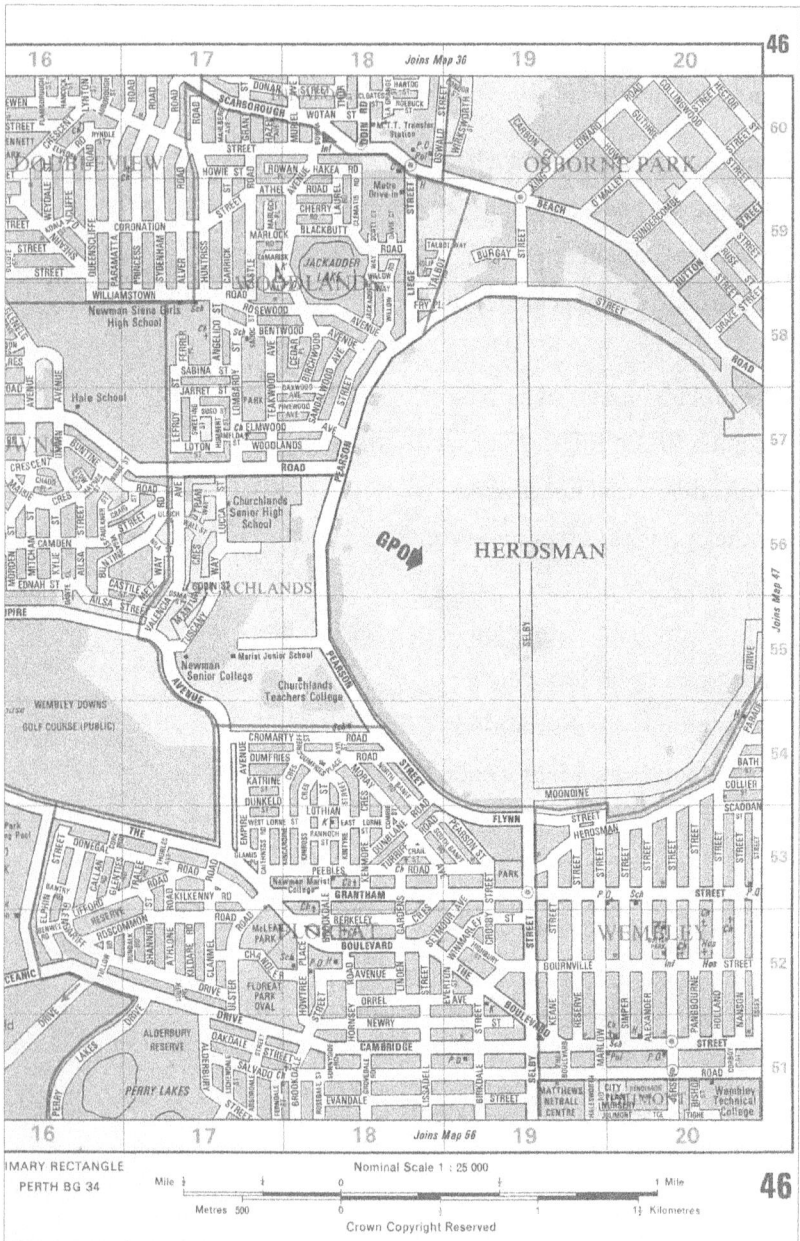

Metropolitan Street Directory, **Map 46, 1978 [3]**

Clearing the Swamp

Early each morning you pull on
stiffened pants, tannin-stained shirt,
slip back into the hole you climbed out of yesterday.

Yanget and cumbungi
have grown back overnight;
severed shoots have crawled out of their roots
to mock the blade and hand.
Black-mired fingers grip your trousers,

drag you in up to your thighs.
Mosquitoes and leeches devour you,
tiger snakes wait coiled,
for a mouse or frog or a hand
grasping a hoe.

From an island of reeds
something screams.
You drop your shovel,
leaving a pair of mud-caked boots,
in the wake of the brown bittern's cry.

Herdsman Lake, 1904 [4]

Njookenbooroo

Mr R. N. Stubberfield 1898, gardening and bee keeping; potatoes – 12 ton
to the acre, lettuce 2–3 lbs each.

Leonard Easton [4]

Eighteen days after hard seeds
are pressed into the sloe
stringline straight drills of hot
pink radishes are ready to pull.

Potato hedges wilt at midday,
resurrect themselves at dusk;
their porous white stones
shove clumpy holes in the peat.

Bees heft pollen
from stamen to petal,
and head back to the hive
fully laden with love.

All night the heads of lettuce
absorb the moonlight,
rows of green lanterns
illuminate the black earth.

Mr. J. S. Collins 13 acres, poultry farm, fifty birds per quarter acre, flock of 550 laying hens and 1000 pullets.

Dawn has barely struck their cages
before the hens are marching
their hard toes out onto the acre.

A scattering of grain, beaks like pincers
they fossick up the history
of the Quaternary sediment,
the skeletons of the food chain,
the dormant fleas.

By noon the birds
are speckled shrubs implanted
in the damp ground.

From beneath the broody hen
tiny chicks emerge;
already full of knowing,
scratching at the earth.

16 dairies in Osborne Park, 1913. Fodder grown in swamp. William
Edward Robinson "Teddy Bobby", dairyman 1905. By 1931 he had a herd
of 180 cattle and ten horses for farm and delivery work

A meandering pad from dairy to lake edge
laid down by the rhythm of udders
swinging towards feed troughs, buckets, strong hands.

Treat her mean and she'll shit in the pail,
sing to her and your pasture will return as cream.

In spring a whole new lake is rising:
lucerne, capeweed and burr.

Camouflaged in white and black
wagtails hitch rides on bovine backs.

Three other farmers were the Guelfi brothers who held 7 and 1/2 acres
consisting mainly of swamp land in Njookenbooroo Swamp. Their land
was very fertile as shown in the results of the 1912 season, when with half
the property under tomatoes they sold 800 cases ... plus 5 tons of inferior
quality tomatoes to the sauce factories.

Bamboo canes weave a threshold
along rows of lake bed unused to exposure,
glinting with black silicone, reflecting
the hope of a first season.

Morning and evening and in between,
workers hawk baskets,
hands dyed green with leaf dust,
sweat running green. It's tomatoes:
on bread for breakfast,
tomatoes with meat for lunch,
tomatoes sauced with rice for dinner.

All night behind closed eyes
tomatoes are falling, tumbling, rotting underfoot.

In winter time the runnels flow
and footprints fill with water.
Farmers skiff their boat and oars,
harvest fish in place of verdure.

Flooding in a market garden beside the Swan River *[5]*

Fong Gow

At night I hear a horse galloping through the garden.
Panic needles my ribs. I imagine tended rows
trampled to pieces under its hooves.

When I run onto the allotment
the vegetables are intact, mutely
squatting in the swampy turf;
the horse is a shadow dozing in its yard.

In the other country my wife will be planting rice,
the daughter I begat but have never seen strapped to her back.
Every five years a visit home and another child is introduced:
this is your daughter.

Forty-five summers;
I tear strips of bark to shade seedlings,
shoulder yoke and watering cans;
the sun bakes the earth into a black scab,
burning the last traces of quangdong
from the soles of my feet.

My long queue is grey.
All night a horse gallops through the field
of my body, chasing my blood
through arteries and organs,
through the bind of two countries,
never arriving home.

Chinese market gardener, South Perth (name not recorded) *[6]*

Catherine Kelly

Aboard the *Mary Harrison*,
bantling concealed under petticoats,
Catherine leans against the deck rail,
retching her way from the Cape
of Good Hope to Fremantle.

In Perth she crosses the workhouse yard
to the corrugated privy; squats over
the pit hole, pressing her arms
into the looming mound of her stomach.
The baby slips

out, a parachutist at the end of the line,
silks furled, umbilical full length
soundlessly plummeting
without one inhalation
into the soft cushion of human waste.

Catherine stuffs her bloody skirts and rags into the hole
fermented space; returns to the kitchen stove,
wet hands pushing the slump of her belly
back into its empty cavity.

The Night Man's Wife

He leaves my bed around midnight;
as his body warmth dissipates
I keep sensing his shape curled into me.
Around the quiet enclosures of shadow and sleep
his footsteps fall in sync with horse breath
and wheel rut, crimping back lane weeds.

I dream him in black and white
moving through the town
with his hat rim turned down;
like a priest he knows too much
of everybody's business,
of the intimate secrets that lurk
inside the hooded cans.

His children rarely see his face;
before dawn he is back, creaking
harness and rusted gate, he slips back into
his body's indent, a faint trace of his night's work
lingering in the sheets.

House of Mercy

By 1898 seventy girls had been reclaimed.

A. Porter [5]

Children are swelling inside the bodies
of barefoot girls who leave their tracks in the sand
up the slow hill to the end of the street.

The distance between birth and birth is a skipping game
turning faster and faster, *my mother said that I never should
play with the gentlemen in the wood ...*

The sheets are clean, the girls' hands raw,
buckets spill black water on the floor
and out into the yard, down the unmade street,

a dark trickle where the sand is so brightly white,
so overexposed in the brittle light.

The Earth Closet

By 1971 there were no earth closets left in Perth city.

Leonard Easton [4]

Some days it feels like I'm dying:
take me down to the back yard,
my feet soaked in the long grass,
scents of wormwood and lemon.

Along the rows of gardens
we're all doing the same parade;
beginning before dawn,
a handful of wood ash, one of lime,
sluice my bloody rags in with the rest.

Water pools against the back fence
where rhubarb grows so well.
Our swallowed words rise up
like undigested bones
as we line up for our turn
outside the blistered door.

The Newcomer

The Maylands Local Board of Health was asked to attend to the removal of some 'very undesirable characters' camped in the swamp further down Guildford Road.

J. L. Ford, letter, 1918 [4]

The sky is too high and too blue;
at night southern constellations turn;
even they don't speak her language as she lies
beneath the roof of her raw-timbered house.

Cold hours descend, diffusing the space
between air and water. At the end of her garden
the lake fringe is blurred by green canopies,
grey bark stripped to the shoreline.

At dawn she can smell wood smoke,
hear children shout, dogs bark,
birds whose songs sound as though they're crying.

When there is a knock at the door she sits very still.
Pretending she is deaf, she imagines *Mrs Constable
in her Garden*, paints herself into the scene,
presses hard against the frame.

Camp at Herdsman Lake, 1904 *[7]*

Camp at Lake Monger, 1923

Silent Morning

Charile Ariti noticed that bird numbers fell dramatically around the end
of the 1950s. He judged that this may have been related to the spraying for
Argentine Ants. He and others believe the bird numbers today are far less
than in earlier days.

Oral Histories of Wanneroo Wetlands [6]

Without the morning alarm
of magpie, crow and wattle bird,
the sun volleys against walls and curtained windows,
the somnolent dream on in their beds.

Down at the swamp:
water boatmen don't row their morning regatta,
dragonflies are not hovering in webless spaces.

Opaline droplets coalesce with water,
gather in reed beds,
drift through the wire of chicken pens
and settle on lawns.

Morning's orchestra is deaf and mute,
tuned to an inaudible pitch.

Yarning Circle

Cockburn Wetlands Education Centre, October 2010

We lived in a wet world
swallowed straight from its sandy chine;
our underwater visible through
membranes of pupil and weed;
our skin as lake, rich, edible, microscopic.
Beneath aquatic, forgetting being human,
our fluids were osmosed to pond water.

We grew up that way:
tadpoles turning into frogs
turtles on the march in wobbly lines,
secret clutches of pale green eggs.

We were raised on mud:
up to our knees, blackening our faces
we smelt as it smelled, sweet and decomposed.

A swamp harrier hovered above our shoulders,
its sight line beyond the edges of our world:
our metamorphosis happened amongst the reed beds,
our flight so brief and beautiful.

The Watermen

Suicide of an Engineer 1

Charles Yelverton (CY) O'Connor, Engineer in Chief of Western Australia,
1891–1902.

The rider can't be sure
if it's wailing he hears when he sets the charge,
lights the fuse and blows a hole in the river's mouth.

He wonders if it's just the westerly
skirling his ears with salt,
or water keening through pipes;

or the refrain of a cantus firmus country
composed by wind and time and people on foot,
carrying maps in their throats.

With one last thing to do:
Put the wing walls to Helena weir at once;
phrases chatter and babble,
riff, skittle and scat inside him
as he rides down Cantonment Street;
heads south along the beach,
pistol huge and cold in his pocket.

Seeking silence he reins his horse
into the cleaving tide.

Suicide of an Engineer 2

Frederick Lawson, the Engineer for Metropolitan Water Supply, Sewerage and Drainage in Western Australia, 1913–1924.

His first destiny was to be born number eight
in a litter of eleven, a small limbed animal
to creep about the underworld, crouch in culverts
bewitched by the way water swirls
from pond to bucket, to rattling pipe,
spurts from a tap and back again
anticlockwise into the unknown.

He imagines gadgets on strings and wires,
the engine of the earth,
melting rock and cooling water;
redesigns streams as brick-lined
barrel drains, sheared up with trees,
pulsed with a steam-driven pump.

In 1916 he tunnels beneath France
with a hose, a pipehead, and a canvas water bag,
drags the river to one hundred and ten thousand
fighting men and eighty thousand horses.
Pipelines, pumping plant, purifying works and
reservoirs, change course every morning
from Villers-Bretonneux
to the Hindenburg Line.

At the Swan River
he channels effluent into the ocean
but still it piles up on Burswood Island,
filters through limestone, gravel and sand,
and ends up in the body of the fish
now plated on the Governor's table.

The Sunday newspapers are vitriolic,
as if all excrement somehow emanates
from the engineer's drafting table.

Early Monday morning
he is awash with estuary,
his body a nightshirt detritus
lapping against the shore.

Building a stormwater drain, Perth, c. 1906

Riparian Zone, Urban

Where the road's edge laps up
against kerbing, rain brims
a rapid stream in the curve
of tarmac, banks up with leaf litter;
a ragged smear of feathers.

At low points muddy pools
swirl with plastic bags;
paper cups plug an iron grate
in the stygian slit of the drain.

The seed dropped into dust-filled chinks,
by wind or a passing bird,
holds moisture long enough
to unfurl two leaves and be swept away.

The road slithers wide of the river,
hissing into the underground.
Beyond the difficulties of stopping,
a duck and her ducklings step
into a soundscape of roar.

Electric Creek

Claisebrook – Yoondoorup

In the streets of Silver City
a naiad has moved into the fountain.
She guards her water well, falls in love
with the ABC radio presenter leaving
the building at midnight, seduces him
with her seed pod lips, her electric creek;

she slips down her architect designed riffle zone,
dowses bronze turtles that march endlessly upstream,
plane tree leaves piling up on their backs.

She beckons him with the sound of water trickling over stones;
echoing through the Brook Street tunnel,
she utters some Noongar language,
shimmies under the boardwalk beside the café
and disappears into Claisebrook Lagoon.

She desires his child, a partly mortal drop of water,
a creature of the creek but with a will of its own.
With his late night broadcast ringing in his ears

he listens for the sound of fountain spray,
never knowing by whose grace the creek
will or will not be flowing.

Electric Creek, East Perth, 2010 *[10]*

Alfred Stone at Claisebrook, 1860–70 *[11]*

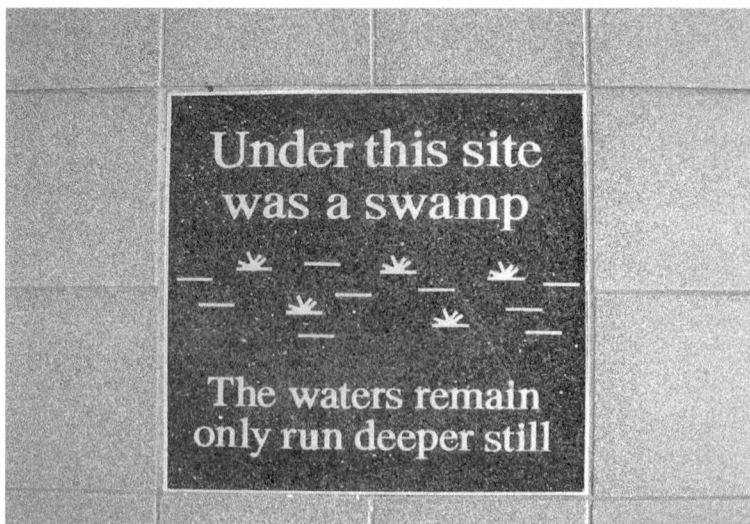

Under this site
was a swamp

The waters remain
only run deeper still

Perth Railway Station, site of Lake Kingsford, 2009 *[12]*

Transit

Site of Lake Kingsford, 2009

A black transit guard
asks a white boy for his ticket.
Boy:
You should show me some fuckin respect
this is my country.
Transit guard asks for boy's
name and address. Boy shakes his finger
in transit guard's face:
Show me some fuckin respect
you are in my country.

The escalator keeps pouring people
onto the concourse. They stream
around this argument and through the tag-off gates.
Trains glide into the station and depart,
their steel parallels laid down
along the dreaming path of Fanny Balbuk,
straight down to Claisebrook
where the channels of ancient rivers

rush through barrel drains
to meet *Illa Kuri,* twelve rocks
standing up near water.

Illa Kuri

Gubabbilup

            Jamoonobing   Boogoorinup

    Goonderup

Gulugulup

                      Goolyamulyup

               Goongarnulynarrimup

       Boodjamooling   Yandigup

                  Doordyoogading

Widdogootogup

    Gogngoongup

Someone has been sleeping here

       on cardboard boxes sodden with overnight rain.

       The sacred dreaming trail is lined with pea gravel,

its edges stained pink with glyphosphate.

       Twelve stones remember twelve lost lakes:

in every photograph of every stone

       the djidi djidi bird flits into the frame.

Walters Brook

*Walters Brook flowed out of a drain which we walked up as lads. We
walked up as far as we dared. They say it ended at Hyde Park.*
                    Interpretive signage, Banks Reserve, 2010

The sound of rain emanates from drain covers
and manholes punched into sandy back lanes.
I follow its rumble, from Hyde Park to East Perth
where it dulls to a muffled mimesis of brook.

Steps in the brick work and a rusting ladder
lead down a locked tunnel I cannot enter.
I lie on the ground and press my ear against
the sound of last week's rain; and on a quieter frequency,
the knocking of a stream against stones,
footsteps of children on an afternoon ramble,
the bass notes of frogs, scrape of sediment,
gurgle as a passer-by stops to quench their thirst.

The brattle of water drums into my body,
merging with the sound of cars passing.
Walters Brook splashes through a circular grate,
where a curved moon of sand swirls into the river.

commune bonum: A common good

The Kennedy Fountain, built 1860 by Governor Kennedy, was Perth's first public water fountain.

Interpretive signage, Kennedy Fountain

Traffic flows around the bay
in the constant curve of Gooninup.

I am wading and falling through a dry pond
the plane tree leaves have blown upon,

empty bottles and cigarette packets
drown in autumn's shedding.

The fountain pool is full of trees
the copper pipe verdigris.

Swallowed back into the hill
the chine spouts weeds instead of water.

Washing Lane

Site of Mews Swamp

1.
The work is hard;
it grabs his face and pinches it,
drags his focus inwards,
squinting into a mobile phone screen.
15 minutes of sun on a concrete wall,
suck down 4 cigarettes.

There's the work,
there's the thinking about the work,
and the work about the thinking.

2.
In Money Street a man in a glass-fronted office
leans into his computer screen, the image splits
and merges: a house, some land, a lifestyle for sale.

Up Washing Lane, two Noongars wander in the autumn sun.
Cutting back along Money Street, I see them
like a mirage heading south, barely perceptible
in the emptiness of the laneway.

Hydrology

Only the wading birds remember
the hydrology of the oval.
We walk our dogs, kick soccer balls,
practise golf swings across this low-lying place
where dawn mist still seeks to connect and transpire.

The lake is pressed beneath
night soil, fish bones, offal,
glass and metal, all our temporality.

Underground the tide retreats to the west.
The oval is mown and fertilised.
Bore holes spit rusty mnemonics
early on summer mornings
when the ibis return to probe this dampland
with their sharp beaks.

Cranes

Fiona Stanley Hospital

Seven tower cranes
roost beside the freeway,
a weft of rooms and holes,
crenellations in bird space.

From every compass point
these cranes are a new migration,
they stalk their quarry, swing
yellow necks above our transit.

Soon we don't notice them,
their long legs quickly outgrow banksia woodland,
cockatoo flight path, the interior
of the egg within the nest.

Soon we no longer hear the birds above
the wailing siren of our own emergency.

Watts Road Lake

Filled and developed for housing in 1987

Straggling behind on a morning bike ride,
I watched the heron morph
from hunter to hunted.

My friends returned to find my bike wheel spinning
on the pavement, my body covered
in dew, rolled down the grassy embankment
to the edge of the reeds where the heron's
flight shadow painted a dark torsade upon the water.

Coming back now; the roads turn in loops
and end in cul-de-sacs.
The street names are an anamnesis to wetlands:
Old Lake Grove, River Bed Place,
Canning River Garden, Billabong Cove,
Foreshore Entrance, Waterside Retreat.

Drain

Drain: a continual loss, demand, expenditure. A tube or wick for draining an abscess. A channel or pipe along which liquid drains.

SOED

While rain makes the earth aquatic,
drowns the slabs of half built houses,
blurs the horizons of unfinished rooms,
and sewer pipes not yet connected;
we crawl through a manhole into the underground;

tunnel beneath the embryonic suburb
where all the nights of the future
are plumbed to pour away
from bodies stripped of suits and dresses,
sweat and love and childhood diseases:
a cloacae maxima of blood and faeces,
flushed into a white splash hole.

But for now we are running bent double;
our screams tear around corners, reach the junctions ahead of our feet;
we huddle in the halo of our cigarettes, under the s-bend of our echoes,
our whole lives poised above our heads.

The Collector

He walks the blocks of Northbridge
eyes down, for a glimpse of the night before.
Between Newcastle and Brisbane streets,
a broken chain, a crucifix, the sheen of a small pearl
embedded in the lip of the street.

His kitchen table bows
under a wunderkammer of misplacements —
gold rings and silver bracelets,
strings of beads, assorted keys —
so that his house leans south-west,
its foundations sinking into an arcanum recollection
of black water and mosquitoes.

He always carries a few reliquiae in his pockets,
rolls them between thumb and finger,
the minerals reassuring: stops short of collecting
the raven, crumpled on the footpath,
eye shining like a dark jewel.

The TBM Operator

Mitsubishi Tunnel Boring Machine

Zipped into an orange suit,
he shifts levers and limbs,
breathes through a tube and descends
deeper into the mud where all life
unfolds inside vaults of limey shell.

All day he gobbles earth and fossil,
moults tunnel segments like snake's skin.

In the cab his mobile phone
wears itself out searching for a signal.
Face lit by torchlight he lunges forward
forfeiting the surface, the weight of the city,
he encounters his origin as a single pulse
thudding inside an airless cavity,
blood-black, wet and heaving.

Pelicans

Lake Monger – Galup, 1920s

What is this coming of argent?
A flotilla of flying boats
sailing west to east, dark motif

splashed on their wings,
noses sharp and unwieldy,
divining rods seeking fish.

Each quiver of membrane is knowledge;
which lake is brimming with minnow,
which is bristling with guns and spears?

To eat and be eaten is a kind of purpose,
a reason to float with the prevailing wind,
to scupper the surface with a thrumming of wings
to bleach the sky with an eclipse of white.

The Swan River Warrior

The skeletal remains of an unknown Aboriginal Warrior found in 2006,
200 metres west of Robertson Park in Carr Street. Noongar Elders decided
to relocate the remains to Boojoormelup (Robertson Park) because of its
close proximity to where the remains were found. Noongar Elders wish
that the warrior's spirit is allowed back into the dreamtime, that the
dreamtime spirits will welcome him back home here at Boojoormelup, a
listed Aboriginal sacred site.

Interpretive signage, Robertson Park

An old man in shorts and thongs
lives in the asylum of the AIDS memorial,
his turbid hair curls like smoke
above a nicotine-stained beard.

In the afternoon he cooks up a feed on the free gas barbecue:
kids dart on the tennis court,
their red and blue shirts flash like feathers
their cries plummet into the nets.

At the edge of the park the swinging arm
of a wrecking ball sweeps back and forth
punching holes into memory:
some bones in the backhoe bucket
bound up in sand and funeral ashes,
shock the workers in fluorescent vests.

The unknown Swan River Warrior
is reburied here beneath a marri tree
where a wattle bird intones its apologue,
adapts to the base and thrum of combustion engines,
the thwack of tennis balls
and shouts of English language.

Old Bottle Yard Site, Robertson Park

Is the grevillea bush dancing
and singing through the old bottle yard?
Suddenly New Holland honey eaters
shoot out from quivering foliage,
yellow and black missiles
whistling loudly past my head.

Cut and Paste Lake

Lake Monger—Galup

Galup

Swamp paperbark, stamens united in bundles. **Swamp banksia**, fine tendrils, densely packed, spirally arranged balls of sophisticated knitting. **Swamp sheoak**, tolerant, thick and fissured. **Flooded gum**, persistent seed pods, wide girth, riparian fringe. **Balga**, peculiar lily, flower compass, nectar drink. **Rushes**, stabilising, breathing stem wave action. **Tea-tree**, woody fruit, liberated seed, particles of sun. Stoop amongst the reeds, knees in mud, lips to water. The men and women outside their huts shake our hands, good morning Yellagonga's family. He's an old man with a spear quivering in a spear thrower, until he sees the gun.

Drain

1909; an incision into the south side of the lake known as 'drain'; a lacustrine decrescendo into the Swan River.

Into produce

Fat cows tread the lake shore into a minefield of hoof holes and twisted ankles. Mud-built wedges appear on the soles of boots. The heron amongst the lettuces, the duck between the radish, an unfamiliar green hue meets burnt stalks of sedge and reed. Chong You, Wing Yung and Sin Loong in conical straw hats, step between the rows, dip watering cans and spray the lake back into itself.

Into park

20 hectares of squiggling micro-organisms, fish eggs, frogs' legs, twigs and duck feathers. The stench of our birth and the bruise of our death; a slick of dark secrets spread across the sand.

Chironomids

Dust bin man, poor old horse, night soil can, poured into the hole where the reed beds sang, into the swamp where the black swans nest. Tadpoles beached and rotting, blood sucking midges plume black clouds into the air.

No boating/no swimming

Regatta white sails, keel deep surging towards the finish I see blue skies with clouds, I see reddish brown like tea without milk, then deeper down the midnight blue, swallow the black mouthful until I am full, losing my voice into a gurgle. I was laughing, I was winning until I was falling. Below the riffled surface they look and look but I am never found.

Landfill

We all went down to the tip, north-eastern side. One point eight metres deep, even my dad was down there on a Saturday with all the other dads. See what we can find: cardboard cutouts from Cadbury, Letchfords, Sanitarium, we set up our imaginary shops. Then they covered it up with soil, we are walking on it now, all our old rubbish, under this grass.

Mitchell Freeway

The birds are adapting, transposing their songs to a pitch higher than combustion engines. Trees turning back into mineral, sheen on the water as a duck and her surviving duckling pedal the drain. A concrete barrier separates them from mortality. A pelican lands on the freeway exit sign, trembling in the updraft.

Grave

A day out with nets and microscopes, hats and shoes and notes from home; an adventure of the invertebrate kind. Before morning tea a child comes running, Miss, Miss!! Scales of silver, scales of gold, a lake full of fish washed up along the shore.

Parkland

All night drains have been feeding in from the east, the north, bringing road wash, buried creek line, compensation basin run off. In the early morning the lake is spat out onto peripheral lawns; subsiding beneath the day's picnics.

Mud Man (or how to sleep in mud)

Lake Joondalup

The after-party boy has been bouncing
to Snoop Dog, Fat Joe and Busta Rhymes.
Yeah it was awesome in the light
and he's trying to find his way home on hands and knees,
the short way across the swamp,
hard then soft, in places like a pie crust
on the black meat of the water table.

Having drunk all his elixirs,
shed his t-shirt and broken thongs,
asleep neck deep in mud, his beautiful protection,
remembering his etiology: before he breathed air
he was a life aquatic, a multicelled equivalent
almost human, almost reptile.

Dawn brings dogs out barking,
joggers and insomniac walkers
are pointing from the shoreline
at his head above the quagmire,
mud-caked, simply breathing.

Beautiful Weeds

The beautiful weeds are blazing on Clontarf Hill;
yellow, white, cream-veined, purple gold.
New Holland honeyeaters ruckus
in the banksia and tuarts,
and from the summit I can see the islands,
the big ships chugging into the harbour
slicing a trajectory across a steel grey ocean.
Behind me the red rooves of houses
stack east in orderly lines.
Three butterflies are jousting in the bluest air
dusting their colours onto each other.
What better thing to do with your few days of flight
than to wing and collide with your attraction,
to reproduce in the hours you can,
then exhale and subside onto an undisturbed hill,
to lay your exquisite wings down
in the limestone and grasses,
down amongst the beautiful weeds?

Herdsman Lake Walking Poet

He grew up on a quarter acre,
half of which was scrub, encountered
goannas and lizards in the back yard,
wee-loo wee-loo, cockatoo's black wings
swept light from the sky.

When the peat of Herdsman Lake burned
for days, a cloud of ash shaped like a bird
drifted across his yard and fell in spirals
into his cupped hands.
He willed the bones of charred leaves
to hold their form as they rained about him,
wished them into feathers and nests.

Fruit trees sling over fences in a maze of back lanes
where he stalks the rhythm of a phrase,
walks the words left, right, up or down
slipping into the pace of syntax.
After forty minutes, no-mind kicks in
and the poems recite themselves into the iris of his eyes
travel through his body so that
they are there nestled in his fingertips
as he turns the corner for home.

Herdsman Lake – Ngoorgenboro, 2009 *[13]*

The Mt Lawley Wanjina

Ron Stone Park

The boy with the spray can has stolen
the rain and replaced the sky with cerulean blue,
the pindan with cadmium orange.
In the early hours of the morning
he lays the Wanjina

onto the slipway drain where it can't
hide from the stares of strangers.
Stormwater sheers across its face,
exfoliates the concrete,
blurs the cavities of its eyes.

Molecule by molecule it sifts
into the pond where it paints the grey sky red,
smudges skimming water birds,
sinks into anaerobic sediment
in the mud of unfamiliar country.

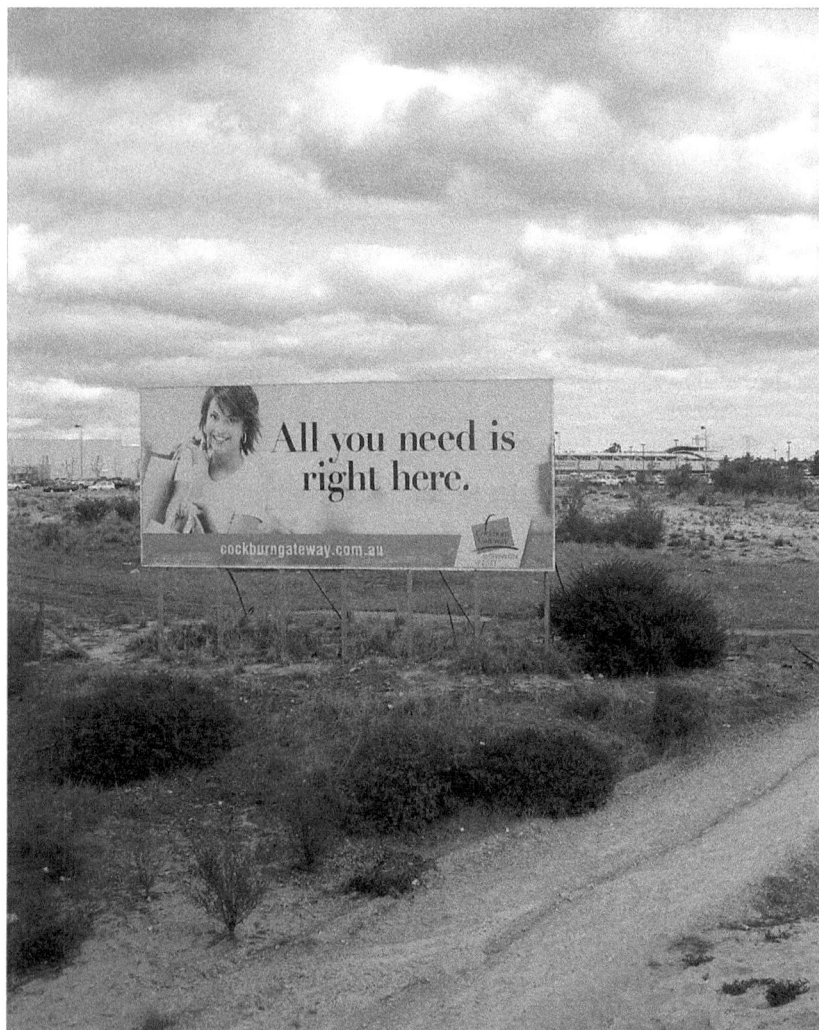

All you need is right here, 2011 *[14]*

Graceful Sun Moth

Synemon gratiosa

Disguised as a piece of sedge,
the graceful sun moth comes at dawn
from the base of wallaby grass.
Her camouflage breaks into fractals of sun
that ignite on stems and seed pods.

She has ten days of autumn
to find her patch of *lomandra*;
clouds passing over mime the night;
she closes her wings, waits for the light.

City as Boat

A thin skein of sand and limestone
porous as a sponge, laid down

by shorelines receding and encroaching.
Concrete caulking and steel reinforcement,
anchor into the rusty belly of an aquifer;

city as luxury cruise liner:
swimming pools, gymnasiums, casinos,
tennis greens, movie theatres, bars.

The UV index soars and cars spill
across freeways mirrored in steel and glass,
buildings shift minutely in the wind.

The city embarks: even the captain and crew
have no idea of the destination.
At night passengers are restless in their bunks,
tumbling into unconsciousness, dreaming the barely
perceptible sound of water seeping.

Dragonfly Lake

South side of Mitchell Freeway

On the map the freeways are green tubes
that plait, touch and part. From the ground
they rise up on muscled thighs like Atlas,
preventing soil and stars from ever meeting.

All day and most of the night
traffic spans the flyovers
accelerating, braking, winding
mobius-like along the on-off ramps.

In the freeway compensation basin,
tadpoles thrash in a viridian crucible
of seed and egg, fermenting in a cold boil.
Dragonflies sew food chains across the pond,
a geometry of light and water.

Mitchell Freeway drainage lake, September 2011 *[15]*

Great Egret Lake

North side of Mitchell Freeway

The sluice gate is rusted halfway open,
revegetation struggles on the upturned bank,
the tree's rough shape and my shadow
stare back from a sepia pool.
I am taller, leaner, a cinematic cowboy
legs astride, poker face, hat looming.

On a raft of leaf and branch
moored under a leaning flooded gum,
a great egret steps, painterly, albescent
in a mood of grey and umber.

Spearing beakfuls of pond,
she hunts alone; turns to regard
my camera-holding moment,

until a ripple in the surface catches her eye.
My finger hard on the shutter, a blur of yellow beak,
lacy scapular, gape sliding fish recomposed in my hands.

Great egret, Mitchell Freeway compensating basin, September 2011 *[16]*

Campanile Tower

Fake Lake, Ellenbrook Housing Estate

The eyes of the tower pick out each blade
in an expanse of closely mown lawn,
telescope into a neat hedge of bottlebrush,
peer into the shadows of the brick pump house.

A panoptic scope across beds of pansies,
reveals a pond; reflected disc of hardwalled
emptiness into which turtles fall, against which
ducklings bump and drown.

The frame is set, this is the action:
a woman passes pushing a pram;
I scribble into a notebook;
a family of magpies guards the contents
of an upturned rubbish bin.

Under surveillance there is nowhere to kiss,
nowhere to piss, no tangled place
to slouch back into animal.

Foragers

Reclaimed swamp—Dixon Park

Through the morning mist the foragers have come,
human-shaped in winter coats, plastic shopping bags
billowing like balloons from their arms.

Gathered around the stormwater outlet,
bending and straightening, they harvest
wild fennel and dandelion,

crush piquant scents,
while all around them straw-necked ibis
pierce the dissolving frost
into a chequerboard of dark holes.

Champion Lakes Regatta Centre

The shoreline is a paisley print
of three-toed stars floating up
from a watery universe made here at dawn
before the car park begins to spill over.
Two red-capped plovers guard the boat ramp,
black-winged stilts pick shallow runnels in the bank.

Bodies pressed into zoot suits
plane the channel, brightly coloured
four and eight-armed corixids.

The water surface is a geometric grid,
two thousand metres, ten rows,
laced with power pylons,
reflecting grey-bottomed clouds;
cut it this way or that
you will come up with the same equation.

Chenopis atrata [17]

The Speed of Thoughts

The dreams of early morning commuters
cling to their faces pressed against
train windows, fogged with fragments of chimera,
standing room only.

Five pelicans glide the surface of the river
on the same trajectory as the train
in which people are travelling
faster than the speed of their thoughts,
towards a city built with thinking stacked high,
with glass reflecting clouds and flight.

The walk from the station platform
is soft on the outside, on the inside
all bone and sinew moving upright,

my body carries me through early mornings
clean and brick, cool with sea breezes laden with rain,
laying down thoughts at the speed of walking.

Anima

It could take a lifetime to study the nature of just one blade of grass, the anima in all things.

Hung Nguyen [7]

The Taoist tells us that clouds prefer endemic vegetation;
that a tree hears slowly so the best way
to talk with it is to plant another tree next to it
and let them speak to each other.

He says we should never cut trees in spring when
birds are nesting, or take eggs from nests,
the shell being both the container and the context;

that anima lives in all things
so we should offer cakes and prayers
to our houses, whitegoods and cars;

Trying to drive home with the empty light flashing,
I place my palm on the centre of the steering wheel,
send all my animal heat into hard plastic,
into the engine still purring when I pull into my driveway.

Dixon Reserve

Former swamp used as a rubbish tip

I am a magpie in the mornings,
winding my tracks into the dawn spoor
where seagulls, doves and ravens
have pressed their braille into the sand.

I'm here for the glint, the sharp edge, the stand-out
of colour splashed against limestone and dune.
My treasures are shards of king brown, the thick skin
of pickaxe bottles, riffled violet of perfume jars,
the ragged necks and glinting smiles of corona.

With my bag and my gloves
I collect blue flowers and windmills
pitted with tea, the pattern of a voyage
rising up through its history, reaching the surface
and jostling for a place with Red Bull and Coke.

The breaking takes place between visits.
Wings heaving, I rise above the tuarts
the dunes, the stony track, the small figure hunched over,
intent on smashing the sun into a kindle of sharp reflections.

Swamp Walking

The Spectacles, Beeliar Regional Park

Down a narrow track fringed by reeds
a small tiger snake pauses,
then slips from the path.

Enter as if through a door,
from electroluminescence
into penumbral eclipse.
There is the bright world of calescent blue;
and then there is the swamp.

Viridine herbage wefts
beneath the pale bark of tea-trees
leaning against angles,
a crosshatched trellis of shadows.

Through this, tannin-stained water beckons,
dragonflies hover, djidi djidis whistle
loud, soft, soft, loud, I see you,
I don't see you.

My skin is shed out there beyond
the circling paper barks,
a skein of shirts and jackets,
hats and shoes abandoned along with
my memorised numbers.

Forgetting,
the ground springs back
leaving no footprints.

Manning Ridge

Calyptorhynchus latirostris, Carnaby's cockatoo

At 6pm
the black birds flew over
so low I could see into
the dark shafts of their eyes.

They were all coming in.
The sky was filled
with what I had always known.
Then everything began to recede.
I was the last person left,
the black bird bursting
inside my chest,
squalling and flapping against my ribs.

In this moment, my learning was lost.
All the taxonomies,
the families, the lists of species
falling one by one
from the hill of my globe.

More than anything else
I wanted the birds
as they disappeared over the ridge,
their cries becoming a part
of the recording of history.

Bird Watching White Fella Style

The PowerPoint presentation
transports us to a shoreline,
where birds stare past telephoto lenses
to a point somewhere out of frame.
Pied oystercatchers plunge their red beaks into mudflats,
a common noddy wades out of eggshells,
nestled in a shallow bowl of sand.

(There are many disagreements
over common and lesser noddies.)

At morning tea we perch around the urn,
pick at plates of biscuits, discuss the sighting
of a tern, a banded stilt, or a red-capped plover.

In the afternoon lined up on plastic chairs
we are shown how to distinguish
an eastern golden plover from a hooded plover
(grey axillaries, dark base of tail).

We learn about the red-necked stint,
which weighs no more than a matchbox
and migrates south in Siberian winters
to feed on the Swan Coastal Plain.
Small enough to fit into a wineglass,

in its lifetime it flies further
than the distance between the earth and the moon.
The chairs are hard,
some of the elders nod off,
their chins tucked into their chests.

As we leave, a wattlebird swoops,
and snaps an insect,
turns its red eye on the car park,
the glistening vehicles,
the strange flock
alighting from the building.

Noctuary

Mary Carroll Park

With forty one hundred lumen of raw bright,
we scan the sides of the footpath,
the black water, the swaying reeds,
the nervous chiaroscuro of tree branches.

In the absence of fur and feather,
we fix our beams on spider's silk
grafting street lamps to grass stems.
We turn a green frog to stone
with the collective shock of our torch lights.

We spot the fugitive mammal, left to roam
beyond lawn's edge and driveway,
eyes wide slits in the dark light.

Bibra Lake (Walliabup) Bird Hide, 1

I walk the tarmac and white line
of a pedestrian's road, gather my harvest
of plastic and aluminium,

take a short cut through the reveg,
a community of canes in triangles,
architecture of green plastic
teetering in the littoral zone.

In the distance the tide of traffic breaks
against concrete kerb and roundabout.
From the shadowy boards of the bird hide
wrens and honey eaters strafe from shrub to tree,
their sharps and flats returning and repeating.

Typha seeds parachute like tiny spiders,
free-falling along the shoreline, destiny absolute:
to survive or perish where they land.

Bibra Lake (Walliabup) Bird Hide, 2

Strips of paper bark, electrical wire,
the innards of abandoned car seats:
are these nesting materials
strong enough to make a poem?

Where to gather filament;
where best to situate it
to withstand winter squalls
and summer aestivations?

I lie down on the hard boards of the hide,
and listen while the avian world
enacts it seasonal knowledge.

How easy it would be to fail,
to have rain seep through,
for the twigs and strings to loosen,
the eggs to tumble, be swooped on by ravens;
swallowed whole.

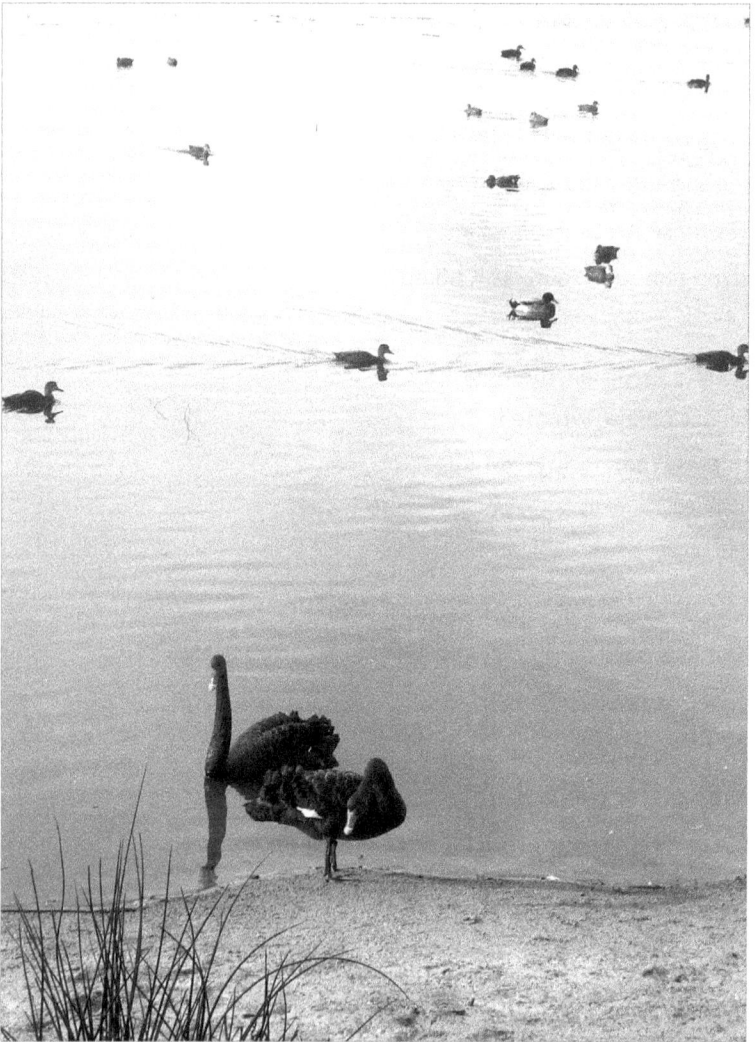

Bibra Lake – Walliabup, winter 2010 *[18]*

Bibra Lake – Walliabup, summer 2010 *[19]*

Horse Paddock Swamp

This font of water
has evaporated into mire,
drawn down beneath the water table,
the lake surface is a patchwork of grasses
scissored by rabbits' desultory graze.

A depth of sediment marinated in lead and zinc,
chromium and copper; stick a match to it
and the whole narrative will burn hot.

A tortoise shell lies in pieces
like buttons cut from a coat
worn when the world was damp,
when you could wade knee-deep
in Horse Paddock Swamp.

Swans on North Lake – Coolbellup, at dusk, 2009 *[20]*

Looking for Shirley Balla

Shirley Balla Swamp, Banjup

Traipsing in search of Shirley Balla:
a bandicoot darts across the path,
rabbits disappear into shadowy tunnels,
xanthorrhoea shed their trunks like jester's frills.

Lost along the firebreaks,
flowers burn like lanterns
from the pocked skin of banksia trunks.
A wattlebird moves through its repertoire
from scream to melody, and Shirley Balla
is hard to trace without charts or compass, landmarks
or shorelines to define an edge.

I find her slumped inside a fringe of melaleucas;
a whole car disassembled in her bed, VB cans
and Kentucky Whiskey bottles litter her periphery.

Arterial traffic noise situates us in time and space,
while somewhere beneath my feet
Shirley Balla clenches her fists.

Frog Swamp

In the dense limbus we lose our way
amongst papery trees and knee-deep grass,

then stumble across a tannin-red stage
draped with melaleuca,

mist falling from the white sky.
A black swan and five cygnets

appear linked from beak to tail feather,
moving across the lake like a showground ride.

Our footprints brim over in the dark mud
and disappear. A frog ensemble
intones a swamp postlude.

The Fish

Kings Park

1.

The fish coruscates the translucent green
of the euphotic zone like a torch in the dusk light.
Exactly which ocean it splashes in
I do not know, as all oceans collide
and wash particles of one country
into the orbit of others.

2.

I do not know who caught the fish,
or whether they exchanged its weight for silver.
When the fish and I meet, it is far from home
travelling in a caravan from gig to gig
like some almost famous rock star.

3.

The sky is clear and moonlight pours
through the knotted lace of trees.
The fish does not feel the cold,
stacked in icy whiteness,
wrapped in plastic for hygiene.

4.

I stand outside the caravan in my winter coat.
For ten dollars the fish is mine, hot and oily,
sprinkled with sea salt.
I carry my fish through the thousands of people
waiting in the park. The stage lights up.
Everyone begins to clap and cheer
as my fish and I take our places.

Stones

Herdsman Lake – Njookenbooroo

The lake's surface is lightly riffled
by a melalueca-sifted breeze,
by sacred ibis purling white,
spiritus asper descending.
A chain of dark pebbles
forms stepping stones between strandlines
until the stones upend themselves,
grow necks and beaks, become swans.

Estuary

The history of water lies open
at page 17, discarded on the floorboards
along with pens and post-it notes.

I grab a coat and head to the inlet.
Along the road, two walkers in new rain jackets
and British accents warn me,
there is a terrible stink down there
someone should do something about it.

I press on past street trees and lawns,
into dunes grafted with spinifex.
On the mudflats scores of wading birds
tread the line between earth and water,
mixing the two with their beaks;

swans plunge their hosepipe necks
into the briny estuary. A small tin boat
is welded to the grey steel of water.

I wonder if the people in the boat can see me
as I squat on the sand, add my scent
to the smell of life.

Point Walter Spit

*Now we toss the sand into the river, now the river knows us, now we have
stepped towards Noongar country.*

Marissa Verma [8]

Lined up along the spit
we bend into the longshore drift,
scrape etoliate fingers into the sand,
rub the wet riverbed into our palms.

We are aging now, and dressed in sensible shoes and coats.
We are longing to know what the river might say,
or what we might hear if we make this small bow
kneeling into the lee of the sand bank,
if we scatter these aeolian particles into the moving tide,
and meet them in the returning wind.

Where the fingers have gouged,
a shell of memory remains in the sand,
just moments before the next wave
breaks into that territory where the country
has met the person for the first time.

Precipitation Cycles

How can I call it mine when its fate is to run through rivers and living bodies.

Barbara Kingsolver [9]

Weary of packing its bags,

lugging its suitcases of dust and river

from harbour to harbour,

drifting between ocean and continent,

it falls when least expected, drenches children walking to school,

arrives in the night to steal the tents and pots and pans

of people camped in dry creek beds.

Droplets pelt into a mountain,

bend and twist, pick up mud and deposit it again,

are dragged together by gravity,

slapped up against the weight of salt.

They swim into the stomach of a whale

and are blown out into solar refraction.

Travelling upon the wind road

they pass in and out of our deepest intimacies.

Turn on the tap

and we are drinking the urine of dinosaurs.

We are rain walking;

falling into crevices,

into the spaces between a life span,

returning to the sky as we breathe out.

Willem de Vlamingh's ships with black swans,
at the entrance to the Swan River, Western Australia, 1726 [21]

Swan River Canyon

*Australia's largest canyon, larger than the Grand Canyon, lies 45 km west
of Perth, carved by the ancient path of the Swan River.*

Amy Middleton [10]

Before the river had a name,
before there was a person to name it,
it swallowed itself whole, pebble teeth
and scouring palate eating the miles
that were not yet miles, excreting alluvium,
building a country onto the end of its tongue.

Submerged mountains sheer into opaque shafts
where galaxies of shrimps glow in mobile constellations.
Deep-sea squid strobe their blue lights.
Starfish weave themselves into baskets.
Crustaceous spiders scutter in rock dust.

One hundred atmospheres deep
crevices wait for creatures not yet invented
to stumble into them and drown.
An ocean rising engulfs an intaglio of footprints
stepped out there when the world was soft,

before the land became the sea,
before the dead were reborn as helical shells.

The Black Swan

By 1876 black swans had almost disappeared from the Swan River. A dredge employed in deepening the river in Perth Water was named 'Black Swan'.

Sue Graham Taylor [11]

Remove the bar and the ocean washes in;
silt and fish scales form new archipelagos,
stones laid like eggs in the soft mattress

of the riverbed are dredged up on the banks
to change the way a river decides
where it will warp and weft.

We call after the black swan:
its image remains on beer cans,
taxi cabs, football guernseys,
coins, flags, and coats of arms.

The ferry plies back and forth;
lancing the platinous skin of the river;
a stone wall seals the terminus,
where black swans once nested
like burnt smudges along reedy shallows
when the river was footpath deep.

Dredge named the *Black Swan*, decorated, 1897 *[22]*

Gilbert Fraser Reserve, Swan River

The wind and I are heading east.
Below in the water all else tumbles west:
fronds of seagrass,
opaque discs of jellyfish
spinning against the pull,
ragged strips of weed,
tiny branches from aquatic shrubs,
all as if caught in a gust,
in a slipstream whirling
beneath my body as I churn
the water, arms like paddlewheels
turning the surface inside out.

The riverbed sifts like fine ash.
Just the brush of a finger
will send puffs of fine silt,
spiralling like smoke.
Tendrils of green leaves
escape from their centres,
like an aerial map of a desert town,
all roads leading elsewhere.

I'm trying hard;

the wind is on my side but cannot save me.

The dog runs along the shore

barking at my spouting snorkel.

I roll in the wash of a boat,

the river beneath me always

escaping my grasp.

White swan in Hyde Park, 1914 *[23*

First Western Australian postage stamp, issued 1884 *[24]*

White Swans

In a hot December
the swans at Fremantle Railway Station
bake like clay in their nests
either side of the clock tower.

Diesel fumes and dust stain their red beaks,
settle on their backs, tarnish
their white wings nicotine yellow.
In winter, storms scour them clean,

pouring off their feathers
and down the stone walls
while we run for the train
our umbrellas twisting in the wind.

Yearly daubings of white paint
transform Cygnus atratus into Cygnus olor:
six white swans that hiss mutely,
necks curved, wings raised
in a threat display.

Fremantle Railway Station *[25]*

The Language of Drainage

600 drains and 29 tributaries feed into the Swan Canning River Park.

Swan River Trust [12]

The language of drainage
has many translations:
brook into culvert, lake into oval,
creek into drain, wetland into road,
Do not drink — Do not swim — This water may cause ill effects.

Seasons and maps of migration
are decoded by the black-winged stint
that arrives from the northern hemisphere
to vacuum the detritus of summer evaporations.
The particular cadences of damplands —
rustlings, clickings, squelchings —
are easily deciphered by the swamp harrier
and tiger snake.

Where the history of a creek
meets the future of a river
these vernaculars collide inside the echo
of a drainpipe delivering its conclusions:
arsenic, mercury, lead, pH 4.0.

Satellite view of the Swan and Canning Rivers [2

Banks to Bardon Pathway

The balance between remembering and forgetting:
samphire, sheoak, melaleuca;
clicking frogs singing louder
than traffic on Windan Bridge;
a black duck perches on the *Private Jetty* sign,
slur of guano piling up on the boards;
the river sheds waves against ramparts
of stone and sandbags.

Sit here for long enough and the river exhales.
Small fish leap from gill to ozone,
and it's a long slow sigh from the opposite bank,
salty and warm, tasting of river weed and sun,
of edges and streams all pouring through.

Sit here long enough and I lose my walls,
pylons, bridges, maps and instructions.
The Swan River is a steady gaze
bearing the weight of its biography,
still excavating its future.

The Eye

At night the river hones its craft,
creaks and groans as it scrapes the hulls of vessels,
tugs at moorings and deposits versions of itself
further and further out to sea.

The woman is wandering along the riverbank.
She stares across the dark mass of restless water;
the light on the automated toilet block
beams constant vacancy from the opposite bank;
a single green eye blinking
through a confusion of riparian fringe.

She thinks she hears a boobook owl
haunting a street tree
but it is only a small dog howling
behind a locked gate.

The rufous night herons shuffle in the pine trees
uncomfortably close to the eaves of houses
where thoughts gather, trapped in ceiling cavities,
isolated from the stars.

She feels the pores of the overheated ground
opening like manifold breaths inhaling,
as cool air falls into the earth.

The Furthest Shore

I leave this at your ear for when you wake
from your sleep of a thousand years
so that you will remember a morning,
a sunrise and a gulp of air. Your body
will recall the swing and stride of footsteps,
will follow these, will know the way.

There will be a faint tune
above the sound of your breath,
and the rhythm of your walking.
An arc of light will filter through the green place
and a voice will sing to you
across a translucent lake so wide it is impossible
to see the furthest shore. You will remember
every verse as if you have heard it before,
familiar journeys in old cars, cold nights around fires
with the great art of stars spinning above in slow increments.

All the words translate into one meaning;
rivers and creeks flow towards that great lake,
a multitude of birds arriving.

Black swans, Andrea Smith, 2012 *[27]*

References – Introduction

1. Solnit, R., *Wanderlust, A History of Walking*. 2000, New York: Viking Penguin, p. 13.
2. Moore, G. F., *Ten Years in Western Australia, and also a Descriptive Vocabulary of the Language of the Aborigines*. 1884, London: M. Walbrook, p. 82.
3. Bonnett, A., 'The Dilemmas of Radical Nostalgia', *British Psychogeography. Theory, Culture & Society*, 2009, 26(1), p. 47.
4. Hirsch, E., *How to Read a Poem and Fall in Love with Poetry*. 1999, New York: Double Take, in association with Harcourt Inc., p. xiii.
5. Cooperman, M., 'A Poem is a Horizon. Notes toward an Ecopoetics', *Interdisciplinary Studies in Literature and Environment*, 8.2 (Summer 2001), p. 181.
6. Brown, L., *Shorter Oxford English Dictionary on Historical Principles*, W. Trumble and A. Stevenson, eds. 2002, Oxford: Oxford University Press.
7. Vivian, G., 'Perth Slowly Devouring its Black Cockatoo Species', *Science Network Western Australia*, 4 January 2012, sciencewa.net.au/topics/environment-a-conservation/item/1155-perth-slowly-devouring-its-black-cockatoo-species.html.
8. Kauhanen, K., Chambers, J. & D'Souza, F., *Report Card of Climate Change and Western Australian Aquatic Ecosystems: impacts and adaptation responses*. 2011, Perth: Government of Western Australia, Murdoch University, National Climate Change Adaptation Research Facility.
9. Cameron, L., *Openings: A Meditation on History, Method, and Sumas Lake*, ed. D. Newell. 1997, Quebec: McGill–Queens University Press.
10. Bonnett, A., 'The Nostalgias of Situationist Subversion', *Theory, Culture & Society*. 2006, 23(5), p. 23.
11. Albrecht, G. 'Solistalgia: The Origins and Definition', blog page, 2008, [cited 17/05/10]: healthearth.blogspot.com/2008/01/solastalgia-history-and-definition.html#links.
12. Walser, R., *Selected Stories of Robert Walser*, C. Middleton, trans. 1982: New York: *New York Review of Books*, p. 86.

References – Poetry

1. Fraser, C., 'Observations on the soil, &c, &c, of the banks of the Swan River', *Western Australian Explorations*, J. Shoobert, ed. 1927, Hesperian Press: Perth, Western Australia, p. 42–59.
2. Stannage, C. T., *The People of Perth: A Social History of Western Australia's Capital City*. 1979, Perth: Perth City Council, pp. 31, 33.
3. Moore, G. F., *Ten Years in Western Australia, and also a Descriptive Vocabulary of the Language of the Aborigines*. 1884, London: M. Walbrook, p. 29.
4. Easton, L. A., *Stirling City*. 1971, Perth: Stirling City Council and University of Western Australia Press, pp. 52, 158–161.
5. Porter, A., 'A Mangle, Wringer, Bowl, Scissors, a Bible and a Prayer Book: The House of Mercy, Perth, 1890–99'. *Time Remembered No. 2*, 1978, Perth, Murdoch University History Club, p. 261.
6. Kennealy, S., ed. *Oral Histories of Wanneroo Wetlands; Recollections of Wanneroo Pioneers*. 1994, Perth: Water Authority of Western Australia, p.10.
7. Nguyen, H., 'Tao and Sustainability', *Tao and Sustainability*. 2011, Rockingham: Hung Nguyen: Rockingham Environment Centre.
8. Verma, M., *Bidi Katitjiny Aboriginal Women's Trail*. 2011, Melville: City of Melville.
9. Kingsolver, B., 'Water is Life', *National Geographic*. 2010, ngm. nationalgeographic.com/print/2010/04/water-is-life/kingsolver-text.
10. Middleton, A., 'First Video: Australian Deep Sea Canyon', *Australian Geographic* volume, 2010; australiangeographic.com.au/news/2010/06/first-video-australian-deep-sea-canyon/.
11. Taylor, S. G., 'Swan River Stories – Dredging', *Swan River Stories* volume, DOI, 2010: slwa.wa.gov.au/swan_river/shaping_perth_water/dredging.
12. Swan River Trust, *The Swan Canning Catchment*. 2009 [cited 18/09/09]; information on the geography of the Swan Canning Catchment: swanrivertrust.wa.gov.au.

Sources – Images

1. Boojoormelup – Lake Henderson, 1864. State Library of Western Australia 3451B/1.
2. Mounts Bay Road, Perth, c. 1870. SLWA 01673PD.
3. *Metropolitan Street Directory, Perth Western Australia*, 19th ed, Map 46, 1978, Perth: Department of Lands and Surveys, Western Australia.
4. Herdsman Lake, 1904. Daisy Bates Papers, MSS 572.994 B32t/Series 9.
5. Flooding in a market garden beside the Swan River. SLWA 050007PD.
6. Chinese market gardener, South Perth (name not recorded). SLWA 050007PD.
7. Camp at Herdsman Lake, 1904. Daisy Bates Papers, Barr Smith Library, University of Adelaide, MSS 572.994 B32t/Series 9.
8. Camp at Lake Monger, 1923. SLWA 54500P.
9. Building a stormwater drain, Perth, c. 1906. SLWA 014087PD.
10. Electric Creek, East Perth, 2010. Picture by Nandi Chinna.
11. Alfred Stone at Claisebrook, 1860–70. SLWA 3245B/14.
12. Perth Railway Station, site of Lake Kingsford, 2009. NC.
13. Herdsman Lake – Ngoorgenboro, 2009. NC.
14. All you need is right here, 2011. Cockburn Gateways Shopping Centre. NC.
15. Mitchell Freeway drainage lake, September 2011. NC.
16. Great egret, Mitchell Freeway compensating basin, September 2011. NC.
17. *Chenopis atrata. The black swan of Australia*, from Hay, J. G., *The Visit of Charles Fraser (The Colonial Botanist of New South Wales) to the Swan River in 1827, with his opinion on the suitableness of the district for a settlement.* 1906, University of California: J. G. Hay.
18. Bibra Lake – Walliabup, winter 2010. NC.
19. Bibra Lake – Walliabup, summer 2010. NC.
20. Swans on North Lake – Coolbellup, at dusk, 2009. NC.
21. *Willem de Vlamingh's ships with black swans, at the entrance to the Swan River, Western Australia*, 1726. Johannes van Keulen, coloured engraving, derived from an earlier drawing (now lost) from the de Vlamingh expeditions of 1696–97, via Wikimedia Commons.
22. Dredge named the *Black Swan*, decorated, 1897. SLWA 230481PD.
23. White swan in Hyde Park, 1914, picture by L. E. Shapcott. SLWA NBHIM00048.
24. First Western Australian postage stamp, issued 1884. Australia Post (personal collection) [Public domain], via Wikimedia Commons.
25. Fremantle Railway Station. NC.
26. Satellite view of the Swan and Canning Rivers. Image from World Wind, NASA, via Wikimedia Commons.
27. *Black swans*, 2012, Andrea Smith, *Alluvium*, poems by Nandi Chinna, illustrations by Andrea Smith, andreasmith.com.au. 2012: Lethologica Press, Perth.

For the Wetlanders – Past, Present and Future

The author would like to respectfully thank and acknowledge the Noongar people past and present, the traditional owners of the country in which these poems were written.

Thanks to my PhD supervisors Marcella Polain and Rod Giblett. Much gratitude to all the people who agreed to be interviewed for this project including Dr Noel Nannup, David James, Stan Dixon, Tim Grant, Sharyn Egan, Mary Dixon, Kevin Gillam and Rex Sallur. Many thanks to Tim Grant for his enthusiasm and website building expertise, Matt Roberts and Shevaun Cooley for poetic discussions, Wendy Jenkins and Georgia Richter at Fremantle Press, Andrea Smith, George Karpathakis, Perdy Phillips, Cedric Jacobs, Janet Blagg, Anne Morgan, Denise Crosbie and all at the Cockburn Wetlands Education Centre, the Save Beeliar Wetlands crew, Leah Knapp, and an especially big thank you to Suzanne Smith for her committment and support.

Thank you to the State Library of Western Australia for permission to reproduce the cover image and the images listed on the previous page.

Versions of poems in this collection have previously appeared in *Harvest, Westerly, Swamp,* and *Landscapes* journals, and in *Law and Impulse: Maths and Chemistry Poems,* the Science Made Marvellous project (The Poets Union Inc, 2010), *Birdlife* (Lethologica Press, 2011), *Alluvium* with Andrea Smith (Art Text Clearing House Project, Lethologica Press, 2012).

This project was supported by Edith Cowan University through an academic excellence grant, and by the Australian Government through an Australian Post Graduate Research Scholarship.

First published 2014 by
FREMANTLE PRESS
25 Quarry Street, Fremantle 6160
(PO Box 158, North Fremantle 6159)
Western Australia
www.fremantlepress.com.au

Consultant editor Georgia Richter
Editor Wendy Jenkins
Cover design Ally Crimp
Cover image State Library WA, 44C
Printed by Lightning Source, Victoria

National Library of Australia
Cataloguing-in-Publication entry

Chinna, Nandi, author.
Swamp. Walking the wetlands of the Swan Coastal Plain / Nandi Chinna, poet.
ISBN 9781922089489 (paperback)
Wetlands—Western Australia—Swan Coastal Plain—Poetry.

A821.4

Government of **Western Australia**
Department of **Culture and the Arts**

lotterywest
supported

Australian Government

Australia | Council
for the Arts

Fremantle Press is supported by the State Government through the
Department of Culture and the Arts. Publication of this title was assisted
by the Commonwealth Government through the Australia Council, its arts
funding and advisory body.

www.ingramcontent.com/pod-product-compliance
Lightning Source LLC
Chambersburg PA
CBHW021148090426
42740CB00008B/992